DON'T LET THE B*STARDS GET YOU DOWN

Summersdale Publishers Ltd
46 West Street
Chichester
West Sussex
PO19 1RP
UK

www.summersdale.com

Printed and bound in the Czech Republic

ISBN: 978-1-84953-576-2

Substantial discounts on bulk quantities of Summersdale books are available to corporations, professional associations and other organisations. For details contact Nicky Douglas by telephone: +44 (0) 1243 756902, fax: +44 (0) 1243 786300 or email: nicky@summersdale.com.

DON'T
LET THE
B*STARDS
GET YOU
DOWN

DON'T LET THE B*STARDS GET YOU DOWN

Sam Dixon

summersdale

You're braver than you
believe, and stronger than you
seem, and smarter than you
think.

A. A. MILNE

!

If you want to be happy, be.

LEO TOLSTOY

DON'T
LET THE
BASTARDS
GET YOU
DOWN

When you come to the end of
your rope, tie a knot
and hang on.

PROVERB

!

For every minute you remain angry, you give up sixty seconds of peace of mind.

RALPH WALDO EMERSON

STARS CAN'T SHINE WITHOUT DARKNESS

Nobody can go back and start a new beginning, but anyone can start today and make a new ending.

MARIA ROBINSON

!

I have decided to be happy because it's good for my health.

VOLTAIRE

IF YOU
NEVER
BLOODY
TRY, YOU'LL
NEVER
BLOODY
KNOW

The best way to cheer
yourself is to try to cheer
somebody else up.

MARK TWAIN

!

Let go of offence. Let go of fear. Let go of revenge. Don't live angry, let go now!

JOEL OSTEEN

EVERY ACCOMPLISHMENT STARTS WITH THE DECISION TO MOVE YOUR ARSE

Smooth seas do not make
skilful sailors.

AFRICAN PROVERB

!

Those who mind don't matter,
and those who matter
don't mind.

BERNARD BARUCH

STOP TWATTING AROUND AND MOVE ON

Float like a
butterfly and sting
like a bee.

MUHAMMAD ALI

!

Nobody really cares if you're miserable, so you might as well be happy.

CYNTHIA NELMS

WHENEVER YOU FEEL DOWN, REMEMBER IT'S UP IN AUSTRALIA

It's good to do uncomfortable
things. It's weight training
for life.

ANNE LAMOTT

We must accept finite disappointment, but we must never lose infinite hope.

MARTIN LUTHER KING JR

YOU CAN'T GROW ROSES WITHOUT A BIT OF SHIT

Comparison is the thief of joy.

ANONYMOUS

!

In a cruel and evil world, being cynical can allow you to get some entertainment out of it.

DANIEL WATERS

TELL YOUR PROBLEMS TO

PISS

OFF

Fall seven times,
stand up eight.

JAPANESE PROVERB

!

Anger makes dull men witty, but it keeps them poor.

ELIZABETH I

YOU ONLY
LIVE ONCE
SO GET A
FREAKING
MOVE
ON

Kick a few blades of grass
over it and move on.

ROBERT BRAULT

!

When everything seems to be
going against you, remember
that the airplane takes off
against the wind, not with it.

HENRY FORD

DON'T WORRY, EVERYONE'S SHIT STINKS

There are two things a person
should never be angry at;
what they can help, and
what they cannot.

PLATO

!

Most folks are about as happy as they make up their minds to be.

ANONYMOUS

EVERY ARTIST
WAS ONCE A
CRAPPY
AMATEUR
(EVEN PICASSO)

We are all in the gutter, but
some of us are looking
at the stars.

OSCAR WILDE

!

The gem cannot be polished without friction, nor man perfected without trials.

CHINESE PROVERB

YOU ONLY
REGRET
THE CHANCES
YOU
DIDN'T
TAKE

Whether you think you can, or think you can't - you're right.

HENRY FORD

!

Either you run the day or the day runs you.

JIM ROHN

IT'S ALWAYS DARKEST JUST BEFORE THE WORLD STOPS SHITTING ON YOUR HEAD

The greater the difficulty,
the more glory in surmounting
it. Skilful pilots gain their
reputation from storms
and tempests.

EPICURUS

!

Here's how to look at problems: Problems are guidelines, not stop signs!

ROBERT H. SCHULLER

PULL YOUR FUCKING SOCKS UP

Hope is important because it
can make the present moment
less difficult to bear.

THÍCH NHẤT HẠNH

!

When thou art above
measure angry,
bethink thee how
momentary is
man's life.

MARCUS AURELIUS

YOU'RE NOT A CATERPILLAR, YOU'RE A TECHNICOLOUR BUTTERFLY IN WAITING

Cheerfulness is what greases the axles of the world. Don't go through life creaking.

ANONYMOUS

Never let your head hang down. Never give up and sit down and grieve. Find another way.

SATCHEL PAIGE

THINGS MAY
NOT BE
FALLING APART
BUT
FALLING INTO
PLACE

Vitality shows in not only
the ability to persist but the
ability to start over.

F. SCOTT FITZGERALD

!

It's never too late to be who
you might have been.

ANONYMOUS

DON'T DRINK THE

HATERADE -

POUR YOURSELF

A DOUBLE

WONDERFUL

AND TONIC

INSTEAD

When it is dark enough, you
can see the stars.

CHARLES A. BEARD

!

It is foolish to tear one's hair in grief, as though sorrow would be made less by baldness.

CICERO

IF YOU HAVE TO FEEL BLUE, MAKE SURE IT'S COOKIE MONSTER BLUE

My only fault is that I don't realise how great I really am.

MUHAMMAD ALI

The greatest glory in living
lies not in never falling, but in
rising every time we fall.

NELSON MANDELA

BRUSH YOURSELF OFF AND KEEP BUGGERING ON

In times of great stress or
adversity, it's always best
to... plough your anger
and your energy into
something positive.

LEE IACOCCA

!

One joy scatters a
hundred griefs.

CHINESE PROVERB

THINK HAPPY THOUGHTS AND TELL THE BLUES TO SOD OFF

Anger makes you smaller,
while forgiveness forces you
to grow beyond what
you were.

CHÉRIE CARTER-SCOTT

!

Tough times never last, but tough people do.

ROBERT H. SCHULLER

SUCK IT UP

OR

SPIT IT OUT -

YOU

MAKE

THE RULES

The difference between
stumbling blocks and stepping
stones is how you use them.

ANONYMOUS

!

When your dreams turn to dust, vacuum.

DESMOND TUTU

YOU DON'T HAVE TO SHOW UP FOR EVERY ARGUMENT YOU'RE INVITED TO

To escape criticism - do
nothing, say nothing,
be nothing.

ELBERT HUBBARD

!

In three words I can sum up everything I've learned about life: it goes on.

ROBERT FROST

MAKE EVERY BLOODY MINUTE COUNT

Events will take their course,
it is no good of being angry
at them; he is happiest who
wisely turns them to
the best account.

EURIPIDES

!

I prefer cynical people. Nice guys grow on trees.

J. MASCIS

IF AT FIRST YOU DON'T SUCCEED, TRY A-BLOODY-GAIN

Only in grammar can you be
more than perfect.

WILLIAM SAFIRE

!

No person is important enough
to make me angry.

THOMAS CARLYLE

FLEXIBLE TREES SURVIVE THE STRONGEST SHITSTORMS

Let perseverance be your
engine and hope your fuel.

H. JACKSON BROWN JR

Don't hold to anger, hurt or pain. They steal your energy and keep you from love.

LEO BUSCAGLIA

WHEN LIFE'S HARD TO SWALLOW, TRY IT WITH SALT AND A SQUEEZE OF LIME

Optimism and pessimism are mere matters of optics... and that can change from day to day.

GEORGE WEIGEL

!

I destroy my enemies
when I make them my
friends.

ABRAHAM LINCOLN

LIFE'S A ROLLER COASTER - TRY NOT TO VOMIT ON ANYONE'S HEAD

Courage and perseverance
have a magical talisman,
before which difficulties
disappear and obstacles
vanish into air.

JOHN QUINCY ADAMS

!

The pessimist complains about the wind; the optimist expects it to change; the realist adjusts the sails.

WILLIAM ARTHUR WARD

DON'T
LOOK BACK
AND ASK WHY;
LOOK FORWARD
AND ASK
WHY THE
HELL NOT

Better a diamond with a flaw
than a pebble without.

PROVERB

!

Cease to anticipate
misfortune - there are still
many chances of escape.

MARTIN FARQUHAR TUPPER

YOU NEVER GET A SODDING RAINBOW WITHOUT A BIT OF SODDING RAIN

Large streams from little
fountains flow,
Tall oaks from little acorns
grow.

D. EVERETT

!

Misery is almost always the result of thinking.

JOSEPH JOUBERT

GET BACK
IN THE
FUCKING
SADDLE
AND PEDAL TO
VICTORY

Still round the corner
there may wait
A new road, or a secret gate.

J. R. R. TOLKIEN

!

Don't get the impression that you arouse my anger. You see, one can only be angry with those he respects.

RICHARD NIXON

NOTHING ANNOYS YOUR ENEMIES MORE THAN YOUR SUCCESS - SO SOCK IT TO 'EM, **BIG TIME!**

No pessimist ever discovered
the secrets of the stars, or
sailed to an uncharted land, or
opened a new heaven to
the human spirit.

HELEN KELLER

!

Be not angry that you cannot make others as you wish them to be, since you cannot make yourself as you wish to be.

THOMAS À KEMPIS

YOU CAN ONLY
HAVE A BETTER
TOMORROW
IF YOU STUFF
YESTERDAY'S
TROUBLES
IN THE BIN

If you're going through hell,
keep going.

WINSTON CHURCHILL

!

If you don't like how
things are, change it!
You're not a tree.

JIM ROHN

DO MORE
OF WHAT
MAKES
YOU
HAPPY

Enjoy when you can, and
endure when you must.

JOHANN WOLFGANG VON
GOETHE

!

He that will be angry for
anything will be angry
for nothing.

ANONYMOUS

KEEP
CALM
AND
CARRY
THE
FUCK ON

Pick battles big enough to
matter, small enough to win.

JONATHAN KOZOL

!

I would not waste my life
in friction when it could be
turned into momentum.

FRANCES WILLARD

TOMORROW IS ANOTHER CHANCE TO BE FRIGGING FABULOUS AGAIN

Angry people are not
always wise.

JANE AUSTEN

!

I make the most of all
that comes and the
least of all that goes.

SARA TEASDALE

BLOODY WELL HANG ON IN THERE

Fight your enemies with
passion and laughter.

EDWARD ABBEY

!

Most of the shadows of
this life are caused by our
standing in our own sunshine.

RALPH WALDO EMERSON

EVERYTHING
WILL BE
SWANKY
IN THE END

It's better to fight for
something than
against something.

ANONYMOUS

!

Be nice to those you meet on the way up. They're the same folks you'll meet on the way down.

WALTER WINCHELL

WHEN LIFE PISSES ON YOUR PARADE, PUT UP AN UMBRELLA AND CARRY ON

While seeking revenge, dig
two graves - one for yourself.

DOUGLAS HORTON

Don't get your knickers in a knot. Nothing is solved and it just makes you walk funny.

KATHRYN CARPENTER

HOLD YOUR FREAKING HEAD HIGH

There is great power in letting go, and there is great freedom in moving on.

ANONYMOUS

!

When you throw dirt, you lose ground.

TEXAN PROVERB

YOU'RE THE
MOST
FRIGGING
WONDERFUL
YOU THERE
COULD
EVER BE

It's practically impossible to
look at a penguin and
feel angry.

JOE MOORE

!

Remedy it or welcome it: a
wise man's only two choices.

TERRI GUILLEMETS

EAT
PROBLEMS.
SHIT
SOLUTIONS.

The road to success is dotted
with many tempting
parking places.

ANONYMOUS

!

Always write angry letters to your enemies. Never mail them.

JAMES FALLOWS

EVERY COCKING CLOUD HAS A SILVER LINING

He conquers who endures.

PERSIUS

!

Pass all the pebbles in your
path and you will find you
have crossed the mountain.

ANONYMOUS

LEAVE YESTERDAY'S SHIT BEHIND WHERE IT BELONGS

The great majority of men are
bundles of beginnings.

RALPH WALDO EMERSON

!

Success seems to be largely
a matter of hanging on after
others have let go.

WILLIAM FEATHER

YOU HAVE TO KISS A LOT OF ARSES BEFORE YOU FIND A PRINCE/ PRINCESS/ MILLIONAIRE

Life is not about how fast you run or how high you climb but how well you bounce.

VIVIAN KOMORI

!

Hold on; hold fast; hold out. Patience is genius.

GEORGES-LOUIS LECLERC

YOU DON'T
HAVE TO SEE
THE WHOLE
STAIRCASE -
JUST TAKE THE
FIRST
SODDING STEP

Life is a shipwreck, but we
must not forget to sing
in the lifeboats.

VOLTAIRE

No one can make you feel
inferior without your consent.

ELEANOR ROOSEVELT

WHERE THERE'S A WILL OF GALVANISED STEEL, THERE'S A WAY

If you think you are too small
to make a difference, try
sleeping with a mosquito.

DALAI LAMA

!

You never fail until you
stop trying.

ALBERT EINSTEIN

YOU CAN'T POLISH A TURD BUT YOU CAN COVER IT IN GLITTER

Isn't it nice to think that
tomorrow is a new day with
no mistakes in it yet?

L. M. MONTGOMERY

!

Success is not forever and failure isn't fatal.

DON SHULA

HATERS GONNA HATE

Pain is inevitable. Suffering is optional.

BUDDHIST PROVERB

If you run into a wall... Figure out how to climb it, go through it, or work around it.

MICHAEL JORDAN

LOVE YOUR FRIENDS - THEY'RE YOUR PROTECTION FROM ALL THE LOSERS AND WEIRDOS OUT THERE

If you are irritated by every rub, how will your mirror be polished?

RUMI

!

Failure is the condiment that gives success its flavour.

TRUMAN CAPOTE

SOMETIMES
THE WRONG
CHOICES TAKE
US TO THE
RIGHT PLACES

(LUCKILY)

If you think you can - you can.

RONALD REAGAN

!

Life doesn't get easier
or more forgiving,
we get stronger and
more resilient.

STEVE MARABOLI

GIVE YOUR DREAMS SOME BALLS

No matter how much falls on us, we keep ploughing ahead. That's the only way to keep the roads clear.

GREG KINCAID

Ever tried. Ever failed. No matter. Try again. Fail again. Fail better.

SAMUEL BECKETT

Get mad, then get over it.

COLIN POWELL

If you're interested in finding out more about our books, find us on Facebook at **Summersdale Publishers** and follow us on Twitter at **@Summersdale**.

www.summersdale.com